TEACHERS
A First Look

PERCY LEED

GRL Consultant, Diane Craig, Certified Literacy Specialist

Lerner Publications ◆ Minneapolis

TABLE OF CONTENTS

Teachers. 4

Teachers

Teachers work
at schools.
They teach students
new things.

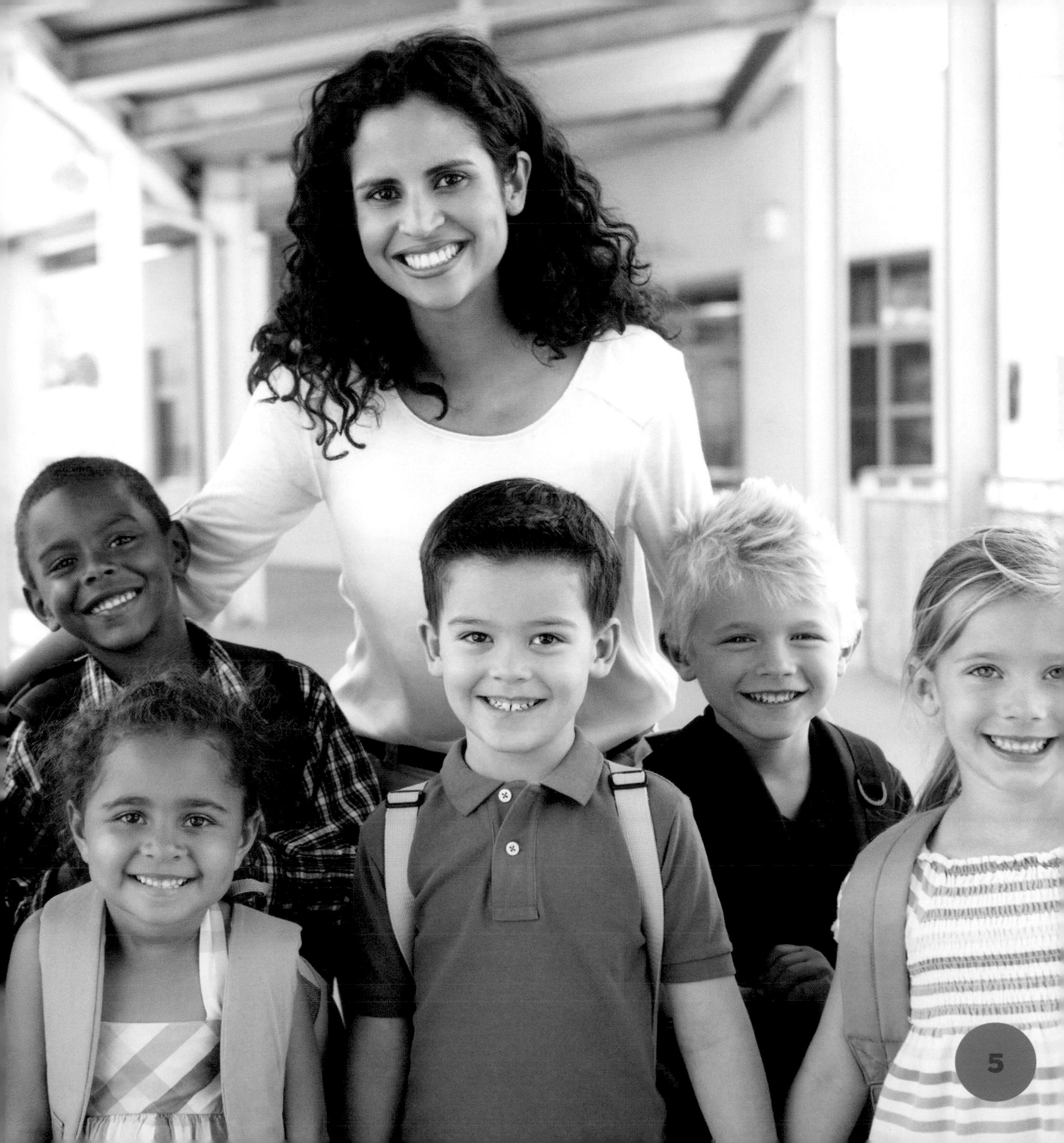

desk

chair

A teacher's classroom has desks and chairs for students.

Teachers help students learn.

They teach students how
to read and write.

Some teachers just
teach one thing.

They may teach art
or music.

Gym teachers often
work in a gym.
They teach sports
and games.

What class would you like to teach?

13

Teachers teach in fun ways. They may use games and toys.

What other fun ways
do teachers teach?

They may use computers
and music.

Teachers work long days.

Sometimes they meet with parents after school.

Teachers go to school to learn how to teach.

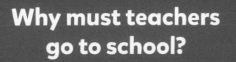

Why must teachers go to school?

Teachers work hard to help students learn!

You Connect!

What is something you like about teachers?

How can a teacher help you?

Would you like to be a teacher when you grow up?

Social and Emotional Snapshot

Student voice is crucial to building reader confidence. Ask the reader:

What is your favorite part of this book?

What is something you learned from this book?

Did this book remind you of any community helpers you've met?

Photo Glossary

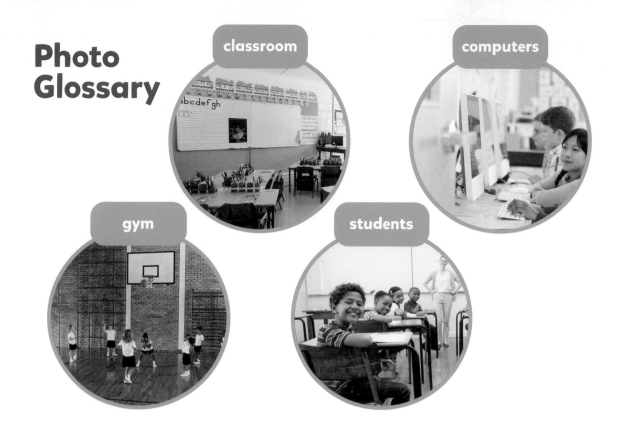

classroom

computers

gym

students

Learn More

Anthony, William. *Teachers and You*. Minneapolis: Jump!, 2024.

Boothroyd, Jennifer. *All about Teachers*. Minneapolis: Lerner Publications, 2021.

Waxman, Laura Hamilton. *Teacher Tools*. Minneapolis: Lerner Publications, 2020.

Index

Photo Acknowledgments

The images in this book are used with the permission of: © monkeybusinessimages/iStockphoto, pp. 4–5, 9; © wavebreakmedia/Shutterstock Images, pp. 6–7, 12–13, 23 (bottom right, bottom left); © Monkey Business Images/Shutterstock Images, pp. 7, 16, 23 (top left); © michaeljung/iStockphoto, p. 8; © anon-tae/iStockphoto, p. 10; © SDI Productions/iStockphoto, p. 11; © FatCamera/iStockphoto, p. 14; © Hero Images/iStockphoto, pp. 15, 23 (top right); © sturti/iStockphoto, p. 17; © Ground Picture/Shutterstock Images, pp. 18–19; © pixdeluxe/iStockphoto, p. 20.

Cover Photograph: © monkeybusinessimages/iStockphoto

Design Elements: © Mighty Media, Inc.

Lerner Publications Company
An imprint of Lerner Publishing Group, Inc.
241 First Avenue North
Minneapolis, MN 55401 USA

For reading levels and more information, look up this title at www.lernerbooks.com.

Main body text set in Mikado a Medium.
Typeface provided by Hannes von Doehren.

Library of Congress Cataloging-in-Publication Data

Names: Leed, Percy, 1968–author.
Title: Teachers : a first look / Percy Leed ; GRL Consultant, Diane Craig, Certified Literacy Specialist.
Description: Minneapolis : Lerner Publications, 2024. | Series: Read about community helpers | Includes bibliographical references and index. | Audience: Ages 5–8 | Audience: Grades K–1 | Summary: "Teachers are very special community helpers. They help us learn new things, like how to read and write. Learn more about what makes the job of a teacher so important in this nonfiction text"—Provided by publisher.
Identifiers: LCCN 2023035557 (print) | LCCN 2023035558 (ebook) | ISBN 9798765626467 (library binding) | ISBN 9798765629581 (paperback) | ISBN 9798765637005 (epub)
Subjects: LCSH: Teachers—Juvenile literature. | Community and school—Juvenile literature.
Classification: LCC LB1775 .L377 2024 (print) | LCC LB1775 (ebook) | DDC 371.1—dc23/eng/20230802

LC record available at https://lccn.loc.gov/2023035557
LC ebook record available at https://lccn.loc.gov/2023035558

Manufactured in the United States of America
1 – CG – 7/15/24